FROM CREWE
TO EUSTON
IN THE GOLDEN
AGE OF STEAM

FROM CREWE TO EUSTON

IN THE GOLDEN AGE OF STEAM

ROD STEELE

First published in 2007 by
Sutton Publishing Limited · Phoenix Mill
Thrupp · Stroud · Gloucestershire · GL5 2BU

British Library Cataloguing in Publication Data
A catalogue record for this book is available from the British Library.

ISBN 978-0-7509-4753-4

Frontispiece: Princess Coronation no. 46251 *City of Nottingham* enters London Euston with 'The Shamrock', *c*. 1955.

Typeset in 10/12pt Palatino.
Typesetting and origination by
Sutton Publishing Limited.
Printed and bound in England by
J.H. Haynes & Co. Ltd, Sparkford.

Contents

Acknowledgements

First, I would like to acknowledge the great debt I owe to my family, for their encouragement and assistance, and to my brother Ken, who introduced me to the joys of railway locomotives.

My thanks are also due to photographers S.V. Blencowe, R.K. Blencowe, G. Coltas, P.H. Groom and Travel Lens Photographic.

Special thanks go to David Loveday for permission to use many of his photographs and to Geoff Goslin of the Gresley Society for his valuable assistance.

Any omissions will be corrected in future reprints.

Rod Steele,
2007

Introduction

A trip to the capital to spend the day viewing the arrivals and departures of the London Midland Region's premier express locomotives was an experience that all steam enthusiasts would love to be able to recapture. Long-gone scenes are recreated in this book in a fictional trip to London from the north of England, taking in a few sights en route.

All the photographs are from my own collection of postcards gleaned from many sources, such as open days and society sales. They are reprinted here in a tribute to those happy days. To the best of my knowledge, the majority of them have never been published before. I hope you will enjoy the book as much as I have enjoyed acquiring the photographs. Notebooks and pencils at the ready. The safety valves are simmering. The engine whistles, there's a little wheel slip . . . and we're moving.

Profile of a Train-spotter

The real age of the train-spotter was undoubtedly the 1950s and very early 1960s, when television had not become the overwhelming occupation it is these days. Radio was at its peak, and our young spotter would listen to favourites such as *Jennings at School*, *Ray's A Laugh*, *The Clitheroe Kid*, *The Huggets* and many other comedy shows. Saturday touched the heights of musical sophistication after *Children's Favourites*, when *Skiffle Club* would play 78rpm records such as Lonnie Donegan's *Rock Island Line*. Skiffle produced many songs that documented the railways.

Boys played outside in those days. Games of football often ended with very high scores, full time only being reached when the players were called in by their mothers to 'come and get your tea before it gets cold'. The only other permitted stoppages were when a signal moved on the railway and everyone dashed over to see what was at the head of the train.

Reading matter included comics such as *Eagle*, *Wizard* and *Beano*, or, if none of these was available, the back of the cornflakes box to see how the give-away submarine worked. Railway books were too expensive for youngsters, so a visit to the local library had to suffice.

School exam time brought an increase in the search for knowledge by skimming through *The Vimto Book of Knowledge* to obtain the information that you felt sure would be in the question paper; the folly of this was only found out after a parents' evening.

Leisure-wear consisted of school uniform, together with cap and satchel, duffle coat and ex-army bag. The blazer was usually adorned with numerous badges, indicating the owner's hobbies. Inside the average spotter's bag would be a regional *abc* guide and another must-have volume, *The Observer's Book Of Railways*. This tiny book was crammed with vital information.

Jam butties and a bag of real potato crisps would be kept separate from the books. Treats included Palm Toffee bars. The banana variety was sticky but delicious.

Where is our average spotter now? Perhaps he is reading this book, and recalling his own favourite moments from the era. Some souvenirs of those days of his youth have probably been saved. Locomotives not worth a second look years ago now draw crowds of photographers, each trying to take a classic shot. How things have changed: in the Golden Age of Steam, few photographers were seen.

The Ian Allan-published *abc* guides were the spotter's main reference book. Always eagerly awaited, the regional versions were published twice a year, while a combined hardback version listing all regions and the BR standards was an annual event. The regional guides listed all the locomotive numbers and the names of each class in numerical order, illustrated by small black and white photographs. Spotters would record each day's sightings by underlining the number in the book.

1. London Midland & Scottish Railway Company

Founding Companies

The route covered in this book from Crewe to Euston has its origins in the development of the London & North Western Railway Company, which was formed in 1846 through the incorporation of the London & Birmingham Railway, the Grand Junction Railway and the Liverpool & Manchester Railway. Between 1847 and 1909 the LNWR took over and incorporated many other small companies. These included the ownership of canals, harbours and some docks. By 1905 the total constituents numbered ninety-two.

Elsewhere, the Midland Railway was expanding its operations by similar means. Formed in 1844, the company was an incorporation of the Midlands Counties Railway, the Derby & Junction Railway and the North Midland Railway. Between 1844 and 1914 a total of seventy-nine companies were absorbed into the Midland Railway.

The LNWR and the MR developed their respective railway towns in Crewe and Derby, with workshops capable of building locomotives and performing other vital operations to sustain the railway. The two companies fought one another for business, as each operated services between London and Scotland. They used slogans to attract the travelling public, with the LNWR becoming known as 'The Premier Line' and the Midland Railway as 'The Best Way'.

Both the LNWR and the MR built stations in London, with the Midland's St Pancras station being by far the most stylish. The magnificent gothic hotel and clock tower exterior were designed by Sir Gilbert Scott and the station's impressive single-span roof by W.H. Barlow. The LNWR's Euston Arch made of Yorkshire stone was intended to impress travellers but it could not compare with the grand exterior of St Pancras.

In 1923 the two rivals merged to form the London Midland & Scottish Railway Company (LMS). Other companies throughout the country similarly merged to form the Great Western Railway (GWR), the Southern Railway (SR) and the London & North Eastern Railway (LNER). This quartet was known as 'The Big Four'. The LMS was the largest of the four and was reputed to be the largest private company in the world, with 222,000 employees carrying out a vast array of operations.

The Big Four reigned from 1923 until the end of 1947, although during the Second World War they were under wartime control as British Railways.

On 1 January 1948 the nationalised British Railways Company was formed by Act of Parliament, merging the Big Four. British Railways was divided into four regions – London Midland, Southern, Western and Eastern – and these persisted until the railways became private companies again years later.

LMS Motive Power

There was great rivalry between the ex-LNWR and ex-Midland men, particularly in regard to the locomotives each company had produced.

Between 1923 and 1932 the LMS had three Chief Mechanical Engineers: George Hughes (1923–5), Sir Henry Fowler (1925–31) and (Sir) Ernest Lemon (1931–2). Each had some previous connection with the LMS and all were loyal to the company.

Both Fowler and Lemon were further promoted within the hierarchy of the LMS, which gave the opportunity to introduce a new CME.

In 1932 (Sir) William Stanier was recruited from the GWR. His appointment led both to great advances in locomotive designs and to a great improvement in work standards across the locomotive works of the LMS. During his period in office, which ended in 1944, Stanier designs replaced many ageing classes. His new engines featured tapered boilers and superheating. With the exception of just one design (the 2–6–2 tank), all the classes were very successful and lasted in some cases to the very end of steam days.

Stanier was succeeded by two other CMEs, Charles Fairburn (1944–5) and H.G. Ivatt (1945–7).

The brief Fairburn period resulted in just one new design – the 2–6–4 Tank, which was a modification of the Stanier version. The last LMS locomotive to enter traffic was an Ivatt modification to the Coronation class. No. 6256, named *Sir William A. Stanier, F.R.S.*, began service in December 1947. Its sister engine, no. 46257 *City of Salford*, emerged from Crewe Works in May 1948 but this was a British Railways product.

H.G. Ivatt became the first CME of British Railways and remained in office until 1951. Although he modified several designs, he is also credited with the introduction of three new LMS types. These were Class 2 versions of the 2–6–2 Tank and 2–6–0 tender locomotives, plus a Class 4 2–6–0 tender locomotive. During the early British Railways days thought was given to locomotive design once more, and the BR Standard classes were produced. Some of these were excellent engines while others were less successful, but for the first time all wheels, buffers and boilers were manufactured to standard sizes. In many cases a close look reveals Stanier's influence in the styling. Sadly, no matter how good the various classes were, they would only survive in service for a very short time before being withdrawn by the late 1960s.

Opposite, top: On the formation of British Railways in 1948 the corporate identity was changed on the thousands of ex-Big Four locomotives. This was the first BR logo, which was available in large and small format to suit the size of locomotive or tender it was applied to. Not all engines received the new logo, and some were still to be seen wearing LMS livery even ten years after nationalisation.

Opposite, bottom: The second logo was more ornate and featured a lion astride a locomotive wheel. Again the transfer was made in several sizes to suit locomotive or tender size. This design will forever be known to enthusiasts as the 'wheel and ferret'.

The final design, introduced in the late 1950s, was to see out the steam age. Again, two sizes were available.

Permission to use the design, a heraldic device, had to be obtained from the College of Heralds, but after the transfers had been applied to many locomotives BR was forced to change the design, as permission had only been granted for the device with the lion facing to the left. BR had made the transfers in left- and right-handed versions so that the lion always faced the front of the engine. Eventually the problem was corrected and all the lions faced the left as officialdom had decreed. Whichever way it faced, this logo was particularly well suited to the Brunswick green of express engines, lined out in orange and black. Black locomotives lined out in red and grey also looked very smart with the style.

Opposite, top: Patriot locomotives were classed for financial reasons as rebuilds of the LNWR Claughton class, but the only old parts of the locomotive retained on some members of the class were the wheels, which had fully rounded centres. Other members of the class were of wholly new construction, beginning in 1932. No. 45500 *Patriot* is seen here at Camden, 28 February 1959. This engine remained in service until March 1961. *(L.G. Marshall/R.S. Collection)*

Opposite, bottom: Eighteen Patriots were rebuilt with 2A taper boilers, and (like the rebuilt Royal Scots) received double chimneys. However, the rebuilt Patriots had Stanier-type cabs, which made identification for spotters easier. No. 45526 *Morecambe and Heysham* is also seen here at Camden on 28 February 1959. This engine was withdrawn in October 1964. *(L.G. Marshall/R.S. Collection)*

The Locomotives

The LMS Jinty 0–6–0 tank engine was a development of an earlier 1874 Johnson design. It was a successful design, with 422 examples being produced between 1924 and 1929. They were built by several private companies, including the Vulcan Foundry, the North British, Hunslet, Bagnall and Beardmore. Only one batch was produced in-house: nos 47667–47681 were built at the LMS workshops in Horwich. Withdrawals began in 1958 with a large number being scrapped the following year as diesel shunters were introduced to replace them. Happily ten Jinties have survived into preservation.

Six Jinties were adapted for push-pull service, and several others received Stanier-style chimneys, but otherwise modifications were few. One exception was the attempt to increase coal capacity by increasing the height of the coal rails at the rear of the bunker. Jinties were worked over a full twenty-four hours at some sheds, with crews changing shifts several times before the engine returned to shed for fire-cleaning, coaling and watering in readiness for the next day's shunting.

Introduced in 1934, the three-cylinder 5XP Jubilees remained externally as built throughout their careers. Initially they gained a reputation for poor steaming but the problem was solved by making changes to the superheating elements. In all, 191 Jubilees entered service. One of the class, no. 45637, was scrapped after sustaining damage in the Harrow disaster in 1952. This is class leader no. 45552 *Silver Jubilee*, with chrome-plated nameplate and numbers. In fact it is no. 45642 *Boscawen*. Their identities were swapped when the new no. 45642 was painted gloss black with chrome embellishments to an exhibition standard. For some reason the identities were never swapped back.

Two of the class, nos 45735 *Comet* and 45736 *Phoenix*, were rebuilt with 2A boilers. They were similar in appearance to the rebuilt Patriots. This is *Comet*, pictured in July 1962. *(D. Loveday)*

No. 46212 *Duchess of Kent*, May 1959. Introduced by the LMS in 1933, the Princess Royal Pacifics proved to be a great success. With a huge taper boiler and a good steaming capacity, they inspired the LMS to develop the idea further, which resulted in the design of the Duchess class. Thirteen Princess Royals were built, numbered between 46200 and 46212. No. 46202 was built with a turbine drive and was nicknamed the Turbomotive. Another variation was no. 46205 *Princess Victoria*, which had extra brackets at the rear of the cross-slides. A change phased in on all the locomotives was the replacement of the original combined top-feed and dome with separate components. All the tenders were Stanier 4,000-gallon 10-ton versions, with the exception of no. 46202, which had a 9-ton tender. The only member of the class fitted with a coal-pusher was no. 46206 *Princess Marie Louise*.

Note the change to the top-feed arrangements on no. 46200 *The Princess Royal*, pictured here at Carlisle in May 1962. (*D. Loveday*)

The Royal Scots were rebuilds of the Fowler parallel boiler design of 1927. Rebuilt between 1943 and 1955, the locomotives received 2A taper boilers and double chimneys but still retained their Fowler-style cabs. Raked, curved smoke-deflectors were also fitted. Oddities within the class were no. 46106 *Gordon Highlander* which had BR-style deflectors fitted in the 1950s, and no. 46170 *British Legion*, which had a non-standard boiler. The latter was originally built in 1929 as an experimental high-pressure locomotive, no. 6399 *Fury*, but a boiler tube burst when it was undergoing trials and a man was killed. The engines pictured here are no. 46167 *The Hertfordshire Regiment* and no. 46122 *Royal Ulster Rifleman.*

The original streamlined form of Princess Coronation class no. 46222 *Queen Mary*, shown here hauling the train she was designed for, running between London and Scotland. These were the principal passenger locomotives on the West Coast main line for express services. The first streamlined engine emerged from Crewe works in 1937, to be followed by another twenty-three examples. This streamlined casing was removed from 1946 onwards. Although only ten of the thirty-eight Princess Coronation engines were named after duchesses, the name seems to have come into wide use for the whole class.

This is what the design looked like without the streamlined casing and with the smokebox restored to full round form. Initially the smokeboxes had a chamfered profile to fit the rounded streamlined casing. The cut-away front over the steps of no. 46244 *King George VI*, seen here at Camden in July 1962, indicates a rebuild. This engine was originally built in 1940 and named *City of Leeds*, but was renamed *King George VI* in 1941. (D. Loveday)

No. 46252 *City of Leicester* in as-built condition, with full front rounded section over the steps. It is pictured at Camden in July 1962. (*D. Loveday*)

The final LMS engine was no. 46256 *Sir William A. Stanier, F.R.S.*, which was completed in December 1947, days before nationalisation. The Ivatt modification of short cab sides and redesigned pony trucks were prominent features of no. 46256 and its sister locomotive no. 46257 *City of Salford*.

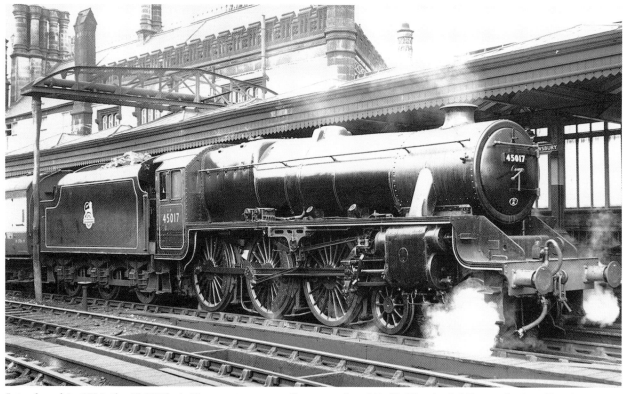

Introduced in 1934, the 5MT Black Fives were eventually to number 842. Unlike the Jubilees, which suffered pairings with Fowler tenders, Black Fives all received the Stanier 9-ton 4,000 gallon version, which suited them admirably. Until 1947 the only difference in design was the combined top feed/dome on some examples. Many variations appeared in members of the class built between 1947 and 1951, and these included changes to bearings, the introduction of Caprotti valve gear, the fitting of double chimneys and a solitary example with Stephenson valve gear. The Black Five design was without doubt one of Stanier's finest. Strong and reliable, they were popular with enginemen, even if they were less glamorous than some other classes. Happily eighteen Black Fives have been preserved.

2. Our Journey to London Euston

The 158-mile journey from Crewe to London Euston will take around two-and-a-half hours and passes through the easier southern grades of the London–Glasgow route. Some features to note along the way include:

Signals and Signal-boxes

Single-post, brackets and lattice-post signals of both LNWR and LMS origin are numerous, and in some locations tall signals are also to be seen. The signal-boxes on our route are those of the attractive LNWR style with brick lower sections and horizontal weatherboard uppers.

Water Troughs and Water Cranes

During the trip our locomotive will have the opportunity to replenish its tank's water supply by scooping water from any of the five water troughs along the way. Introduced by LNWR engineer John Ramsbottom in 1860, the first troughs were laid at Mochdre in North Wales in order to speed the running of the Irish Mail. In all there were thirty-five LMS troughs, and the savings they allowed in both time and operating costs over 108 years of use must have been colossal. Before their introduction, locomotives were forced to stop for between five and ten minutes in order to refill the tender tanks at some stations. Troughs enabled around 2,000 gallons of water to be picked up at speeds over 30 mph over a distance of a few hundred yards. Both LMS- and LNWR-style water cranes are common along the route, although our express will replenish water from the troughs to avoid stopping.

Station Buildings

By far the most attractive station buildings are those along the Trent Valley. Many display ornate brickwork with Tudor-style chimneys and chequer pattern roof tiles similar to some stately homes.

Goods Trains

Ignored by many spotters are the humble workings of the goods trains. Headed by the less glamorous locomotive types such as 8F 'Eight Freights' and LNWR 0–8–0s, numerous long coal trains made up of 16-ton mineral wagons are to be seen on their way south from the coalfields of the Midlands. Also on view are the mixed goods trains with a wide variety of types of wooden-bodied wagons.

Mail Trains

At particular times of day a spotter might see a Royal Mail train composed of special coaches allowing the sorting of mail on the move. Chequered notices on our route indicate the location of the retractable catchers used to gather the sacks of mail into the coaches, again so the train can keep moving.

The Route from Crewe to Euston

Crewe (158 miles from London Euston) ⇒ *Whitmore Troughs* ⇒ Madeley (150 miles) ⇒

Norton Bridge (138 miles) ⇒ Stafford (133 miles) ⇒ Colwick (127 miles) ⇒

Rugeley (124 miles) ⇒ Armitage (121 miles) ⇒ Lichfield (116 miles) ⇒

Hademore Troughs ⇒ Tamworth ⇒ Polesworth (106 miles) ⇒

Atherstone (102 miles) ⇒ Nuneaton (97 miles) ⇒ Shilton (91 miles) ⇒

Brinklow (88 miles) ⇒ *Newbold Troughs* ⇒ Rugby Midland (82 miles) ⇒

Welton (75 miles) ⇒ Weedon (69 miles) ⇒ Blisworth (62 miles) ⇒

Roade (59 miles) ⇒ *Castlethorpe Troughs* ⇒ Wolverton (52 miles) ⇒

Bletchley (46 miles) ⇒ Leighton Buzzard (40 miles) ⇒

Cheddington (36 miles) ⇒ Tring (31 miles) ⇒ Berkhamsted (28 miles) ⇒

Hemel Hempstead (24 miles) ⇒ Apsley (23 miles) ⇒ Kings Langley (21 miles) ⇒

Watford Junction (17 miles) ⇒ Bushey & Oxhey (16 miles) ⇒ *Bushey Troughs* ⇒

Hatch End (13 miles) ⇒ Harrow & Wealdstone (11 miles) ⇒

Wembley (8 miles) ⇒ Willesden (5 miles) ⇒ Primrose Hill Tunnels

⇒ London Euston

Water pick-up points shown in *italics*

Crewe

We begin our journey at Crewe, the Mecca of the London Midland region. Any enthusiast who visits the station will have happy memories of scenes that no amount of planning or money could ever recreate. The bustling activities of this vital railway junction can overwhelm the enthusiast not only with sightings but also with the smoke haze that is an everyday pollution problem in the station. The huge number of arrivals and departures results in a wide variety of locomotive classes for spotters. Predictable sightings include Stanier Pacifics, Royal Scots, Patriots, Jubilees and Jinties. One seemingly never-ending activity for the numerous Crewe-based Jinties is the removal and attachment of coaching stock, although between duties they seem to hide away in quieter parts of the station. Unpredictable sightings include the procession of locomotives going to the works for overhaul. It is always possible to find an elusive locomotive from some remote part of the region. After overhaul, running-in tests produce strange combinations of gleaming, lined out engines running to local destinations such as Shrewsbury. This ensures the bearings are properly bedded in and that all is well with the valve settings before the locomotive returns to its home depot.

A typical Crewe scene. Duchess no. 46250 *City of Lichfield* in company with Jubilee no. 45643 *Rodney* thrill the crowd of spotters on the lattice bridge, favoured by many for its panoramic views. (*G.W. Sharpe/R.S. Collection*)

The Crewe North shedplate could be seen on the 125 engines that were in the shed's allocation in the late 1950s. The many destinations for which 5A provided motive power and men meant that the footplate crews needed vast route knowledge. The depot closed in 1965.

Crewe South shedplate. This depot had 117 engines in its allocation in the 1950s, principally for goods and parcels trains. Like the North Shed men, the crews here needed full route knowledge. This depot closed in 1967.

Royal Scot no. 46111 *Royal Fusilier* restarts its train, watched by several spotters who are doubtless recording the sighting in their Ian Allan *abc* books! At this time no. 46111 is allocated to Manchester Longsight (9A) depot. It was built in 1927 by the North British Locomotive Company and rebuilt with a taper boiler in 1947.

A Crewe product, unrebuilt Patriot no. 45551 passes through Crewe light engine in 1953. Eighteen of the class were rebuilt and closely resembled the rebuilt Royal Scots. This engine was to retain its original 1934 looks throughout its career. It was one of nine Patriots that were never named. (*G.W. Sharpe/R.S. Collection*)

No. 46256 *Sir William A. Stanier F.R.S*, flanked by the next generation of motive power. Although named after Stanier, this engine was one of two Princess Coronation class engines modified by H.G. Ivatt, as was its sister engine, no. 46257 *City of Salford.*

Below: The porters take a break while the crew of Black Five no. 45009 keep the locomotive's safety valves simmering, ready for the road.

Black Five no. 45231, built by Armstrong-Whitworth, waits for the signals to clear. All the doors are secured and it can only be a few moments before the locomotive departs. No matter what form of identification is used, it always spoils the appearance of the smokebox. This chalked method is the worst of all. Sister engine no. 44842 alongside has one safety valve lifting – a good sign that all is well with its steam pressure.

Opposite, top: Crewe-built Jubilee no. 45622 *Nyasaland* glides by, carrying another form of train identification. Again this spoils the smokebox, and frustrates spotters by hiding the number-plate from view. *Nyasaland* was built in 1934.

Opposite, bottom: A common sight at Crewe is the procession of locomotives heading either for the works or coming and going on to shed. Here Princess Royal class no. 46203 *Princess Margaret Rose* is coupled between two Black Fives. This is one of the two members of the class to survive into preservation. (*Travel Lens Photographic*)

Edge Hill-based Princess Coronation class no. 46243 *City of Lancaster* awaits the signals to resume her journey. This locomotive was the last of the streamlined versions to be rebuilt without the 3 tons of streamlined casing. One of the engine's nameplates was sold in later years and cost its new owner three times more than the engine and tender had cost when new in 1940! (*Travel Lens Photographic*)

Jinty no. 47467, a Crewe South engine, awaits its next task as station pilot. This engine was built in 1928 at the Vulcan Foundry.

In this 1952 scene an immaculately turned out Jubilee, no. 45586 *Mysore*, coupled to a Fowler 3,500-ton capacity tender, backs through the station past gangers at work on the track. (*J.W. Neve/R.S. Collection*)

Patriot no. 45504 *Royal Signals* at Crewe in 1952. The tender is filled with huge lumps of coal and the fireman will have to do some hard work with his coal pick to fill the firebox. (*J.W. Neve/R.S. Collection*)

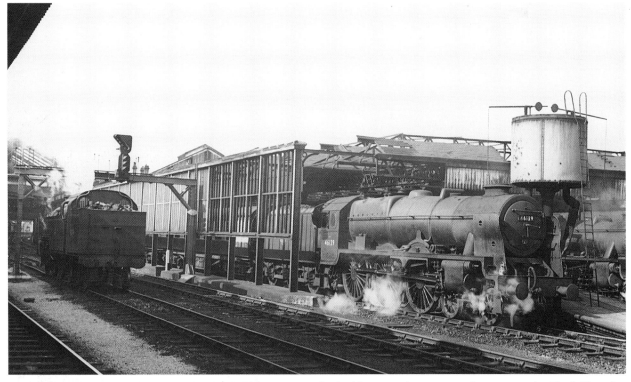

Pictured in 1952, Royal Scot no. 46139 *The Welch Regiment* is flanked by a Fowler 2–6–4 tank engine and a Black Five. An example of the parachute-type water column seen on many platform ends is visible behind the Scot. (*J.W. Neve/ R.S. Collection*)

Britannia Pacific no. 70049 has charge of 'The Irish Mail' train, running from Holyhead to Euston. This locomotive was later named *Solway Firth*. The Britannia 7MT 4–6–2s were introduced in 1951 by British Railways, and were the first of twelve Standard classes.

Jubilee no. 45733 *Novelty* leaving Crewe with a train of Stanier coaches. The Brunswick green of the engine and the maroon stock blend well together. (*G.W. Sharpe/R.S. Collection*)

Bearing the cut-down smokebox of ex-streamliners, no. 46220 *Coronation* has charge of the 'Royal Scot' Up train, August 1951. The lion rampant version of the headboard gives the train a purposeful appearance in keeping with its importance. (*E.R. Morton/R.S. Collection*)

No. 46239 *City of Chester* beneath the gathering overhead wires that signalled the end for steam. Yellow warning stripes are soon to appear on the cab sides of locomotives barred from running south of Crewe. (*Simpson/Evans/R.S. Collection*)

The Crewe North signal-box (now the Heritage Centre) is just visible as Royal Scot no. 46149 *The Middlesex Regiment* clears the station exit travelling northwards. This engine was built in 1927 and named *Lady of the Lake*; it was rebuilt in May 1936 and given its new name. (*Simpson/Evans/R.S. Collection*)

Jinty no. 47450 seen from one of the new electric-hauled trains as it awaits its next duty. Many Jinties can be observed lingering around Crewe station.

Royal Scot no. 46154 *The Hussar* dwarfed by the newly erected overhead wires at Crewe.

Flashback to 21 July 1937. Streamlined no. (4)6222 *Queen Mary* with the Down 'Coronation Scot' picks up water at Whitmore troughs. In the previous month its sister engine no. (4)6220 *Coronation* had achieved the World Steam Record of 114 mph, and was travelling at over 85 mph at this location. The LNER locomotive *Mallard* was to beat this record, although she burnt out her bearings in the process. *Coronation* was turned at Crewe and completed the return journey to London without any problems.

Stafford

Stafford is a junction for Birmingham, Derby and Shrewsbury and offers a great variety of loco classes to observe. Apart from the crack expresses, there is a chance to see rarities from other parts of the country. After overhaul in Crewe Works, engines are sometimes 'run-in' on the Shrewsbury trains. To the delight of the spotters, the elusive Duchess from the Scottish region might appear.

Royal Scot no. 46148 *The Manchester Regiment* displaying a good head of steam and a nice exhaust from her double chimney, 1956. The double-lined version of the nameplate with regimental badge can be seen. This engine was built in 1927 as *Velocipede*; it was renamed in 1935. (*G.W. Sharpe/R.S. Collection*)

Patriot no. 45507 *Royal Tank Corps* at Stafford, 3 June 1952. The road of terraced houses provides a good viewpoint for any enthusiast living there. (*E.R. Morton/R.S. Collection*)

Princess Coronation class no. 46245 *City of London* arrives at Stafford on Whit Saturday, 1962. The tender seems to have been filled with huge lumps of coal, which will mean a lot of hard work for the fireman to load the firebox.

Slowed by a permanent way slack, Princess Royal class no. 46205 *Princess Victoria* gets her train underway again. The young man in bib and brace overalls is the signalman's runner, who will have advised the locomotive crew about the restriction.

The crane in the background indicates that this view was taken during the early electrification period. Another Princess Royal, no. 46208 *Princess Helena Victoria*, is in charge of one of her regular duties, the Liverpool–Euston train known as 'The Merseyside Express'. (*Travel Lens Photographic*)

Tamworth

Tamworth is noteworthy for having High and Low Level stations, and lines that cross at right angles to each other. One of these lines is the West Coast main line, the other the Derby–Birmingham line. In addition, the station provides an interface with postal traffic linked to the day and night mail trains. However, most enthusiasts are more interested in the number of trains that can be observed.

During school holidays and at weekends Tamworth station used to be inundated with spotters, until eventually their numbers became so great that the authorities banished them from the station. Undeterred, the spotters relocated to a field. Rumour has it that the farmer, who never misses a commercial opportunity, soon began charging them admission!

Royal Scot no. 46111 *Royal Fusilier* of Longsight shed (9A) runs through Tamworth station, 5 May 1956. Adverts for Virol and Palethorpes Sausages can be seen below the Tamworth Low Level station nameboard. (*G.W. Sharpe/R.S. Collection*)

Opposite, top: Princess Royal Class no. 46207 *Princess Arthur of Connaught* passes under Tamworth High Level station. In the background is the Royal Mail transfer chute used to move mail from the High to the Low Level station for the West Coast postal train.

Opposite, bottom: Royal Scot no. 46143 *The South Staffordshire Regiment*, with steam shut off, coasts through Lichfield.

The Trent valley proved an ideal location to watch express trains travelling at speed. Once more no. 46208 *Princess Helena Victoria* is in charge of 'The Merseyside Express'. This view pre-dates the earlier photograph at Stafford as the tender carries the early version of the BR logo. (*Travel Lens Photographic*)

Young enthusiasts watch as no. 46205 *Princess Victoria* thunders past with 'The Merseyside Express', a regular Princess duty. Many enthusiasts spend hours trackside perched on bike crossbars or fences, and the flow of trains seems endless. (*Travel Lens Photographic*)

Popular from the 1950s into the 1960s are the 'Music at Midnight Specials' to various dance and music events around the country. Here Royal Scot 46124 *London Scottish* passes Lichfield on 7 July 1962. (*A.J. Sullivan/R.S. Collection*)

Royal Scot no. 46153 *The Royal Dragoon* passes Lichfield signal-box with a Manchester–Euston express, 8 August 1959. (*A.J. Sullivan/R.S. Collection*)

Rugby Midland and Watford

Rugby Midland is an ideal spotters' haunt. A huge number of trains pass through. One platform is so long that it can accommodate trains of twenty-four coaches. Observations include all Anglo-Scottish and Northwest express workings. In later years we may regret not paying more attention to the frequent goods trains that pass through.

Watford Junction is the terminus of the Euston electric service introduced in 1922 by the LNWR. As a change from expresses thundering through, the enthusiast shows more interest in 1C Watford Shed, which lies adjacent to the platforms. The allocation includes some of the early Fowler designs 2P, 3F and 4F, which see service on the branch line to St Albans.

Royal Scot no. 46124 *London Scottish* is admired by a young spotter perched on a very unsafe vantage point at Rugby Midland.

Opposite, top: BR Standard class 5 no. 73033 awaits a clear road by Rugby no. 4 signal-box. The boiler design was similar to that of the Black Fives. Don't be misled by the extra chimneys – they belong to the terraced properties in the background!

Opposite, bottom: A Down freight train negotiates the complex of lines at Rugby behind Patriot no. 45547, 18 August 1959. This was one of several members of the class that remained unnamed. (*P.H. Groom*)

Black Five no. 45127 passes through Bletchley in 1960 with the vacuum-fitted stock of a parcels train. Lineside items include an LNWR water crane, tall lattice signals and a gas lamp.

Patriot no. 45530 *Sir Frank Ree* pauses at Watford Junction with a short train of just three coaches. Rebuilt with a taper boiler in 1946, this locomotive was the last of its class to remain in service, being finally withdrawn in December 1965.

Royal Scot no. 46144 *Honourable Artillery Company* passes Watford shed (1C), where one of the numerous Midland 4F 0–6–0s awaits its next duty, possibly down the branch line to St Albans. This Royal Scot was built in 1927 and was originally named *Ostrich*; it was renamed in 1933.

A close-up reveals the 4F to be no. 44348 of Watford shed. It is one of 772 in the class and was built in 1927 by the Kerr Stuart Works. Watford shed is in the typical style of the LNWR.

Sunlight and shade contrast as rebuilt Patriot no. 45531 *Sir Frederick Harrison* trundles through Watford Junction station with a parcels train. This engine was built in 1933 and remained nameless until 1937. It was rebuilt with a taper boiler in late 1947.

With so many glamorous express-type locomotives to watch, little notice is given to more mundane workhorses such as the very successful Stanier 8F 2–8–0. Here locomotive no. 48248 is seen on a typical goods train at Kenton in 1955. These 'Eight Freights' are a classic design and serve as the principal heavy goods engines on the London Midland Region. The last examples were withdrawn as late as 1968.

Willesden Shed (1A)

With an allocation of 130 locomotives, 1A could fill a book on its own, so there is space here only for a selection of the variety of classes on show. The depot yard seems to have a forest of lighting posts covering the whole of its sprawling site. Although its sub-shed Camden 1B has the cream of the express locomotives, Willesden boasts a huge variety of most LMR engine types. Duchesses, Royal Scots, Jubilees and Patriots are frequently found here, alongside less glamorous but still noteworthy classes. My enduring memory of 1A is of lines upon lines of engines, most in urgent need of cleaning.

Willesden's moment of glory came in 1954 when the International Railway Congress Exhibition used the specially tidied roundhouse to display a selection of the new BR Standard locomotives. This caused major problems as working locomotives had to go elsewhere for turning so as not to disrupt the display. It did not take long afterwards for 1A to return to its normal everyday grimy state.

Jinty no. 47302 passes through Willesden Junction on a freight working. The 1A shedplate reveals this tank engine to be close to its home shed of Willesden.

Royal Scot no. 46129 *The Scottish Horse* amid the new-style concrete column lighting posts at Willesden Junction. Built in 1927, it was originally named *Comet*; it was renamed in January 1936.

Princess Coronation class no. 46255 *City of Hereford* passes under the platform footbridge at Willesden, making easy work of a long train. This engine was built in 1946.

Taken from the vantage point of the footbridge, this is a fine shot of both Royal Scot no. 46148 *The Manchester Regiment* and the station architecture at Willesden.

A nicely turned-out Ivatt 2–6–0 no. 46472 of Willesden shed awaits its next duties in April 1962. In the background can be seen the many vents that allowed the smoke to escape from within the shed. (*D. Loveday*)

Willesden's own Stanier 2–6–4 tank no. 42581 beside an inspection pit in the shed yard. These are versatile engines, mostly employed on local passenger and cross-country services, and they are widely distributed.

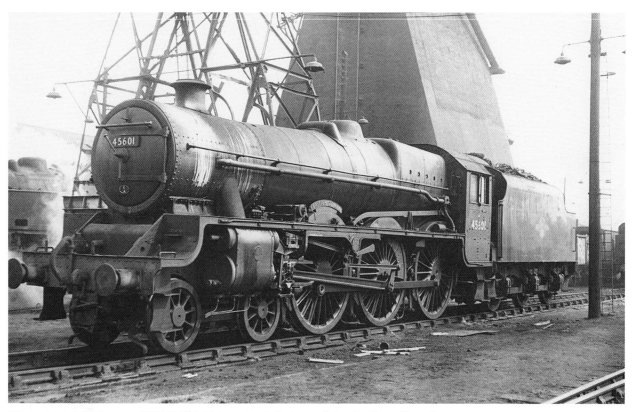

Work-stained Jubilee no. 45601 *British Guiana* stands in front of the shed's coaling plant.

Patriot no. 45547 stands ready for action at Willesden. The smoke hoods in the background give an indication of the shed's size and smoke pollution potential.

Royal Scot no. 46159 *The Royal Air Force* stands alongside Black Five class leader no. 45000. Despite its number, this was not the first Black Five to be built.

When Camden (1B) was closed several 'Duchess' locomotives were transferred to Willesden although doubts were expressed about the crews there keeping them in good condition. However, the men rose to the challenge and maintained them in superb condition, as can be seen with no. 46240 *City of Coventry*, pictured here on shed. Completed in 1940, this engine was withdrawn in September 1964 and scrapped.

Two members of the Princess Royal class placed in store with their chimneys and cabs covered over, awaiting their fate. No. 46205 *Princess Victoria* still retains the brackets from an early experimental modification. No. 46207's name – *Princess Arthur of Connaught* – caused confusion and mirth among spotters: a Princess named Arthur!

3. The Approach to London Euston

As our train nears the end of its journey we can begin to recognise landmarks providing an idea of where we are. On the left is a roundhouse building, the original Camden motive power depot. This Grade II listed building is now used as a theatre. The large Camden goods depot can also be seen on the left. The Camden motive power depot (1B) directly opposite is more interesting. Visible from the line is the north end of the shed, and on view will be an array of express engines facing north and waiting to join their trains in Euston.

The Camden allocation for 1959 was forty-one locomotives, all essentially express types. There were four Patriots, eight Jubilees, nine Royal Scots and eight Coronation Pacifics, along with twelve Jinties for minor duties. Diesels were to arrive later in the year. At the south end of the shed are many more engines awaiting the servicing facilities ready for their next turns of duty.

After passing Camden shed our train starts the last mile of its working by descending Camden Bank and gliding into Euston. Down trains have a far more difficult task because between Euston and Camden no. 1 signal-box the bank varies in gradient between 1 in 70 and 1 in 112. This frequently necessitates the use of a banking engine. The banking engines are sometimes a motley collection provided for station pilot duties by Willesden, or for empty carriage stock to and from sidings. The train engine from the Up working will give the starting train a push and then drop off on reaching the shed approach at Camden, a mile out from the station.

Royal Scot no. 46127 *The Old Contemptibles* is a mile from journey's end, passing the original Camden roundhouse on the Up line, on 28 May 1959. (*L.G. Marshall/R.S. Collection*)

Directly opposite Camden shed Princess Coronation no. 46229 *Duchess of Hamilton* passes the delightfully named Primrose Hill (formerly Chalk Farm) station and begins the last mile of its journey on 28 February 1959. (*L.G. Marshall/R.S. Collection*)

A dream photograph or a spotter's nightmare: no. 46248 *City of Leeds* is charging up the gradient out of Euston with a Down train in July 1962. Going the other way is no. 46206 *Princess Marie Louise* with an Up train on the easier downgrade to Euston. Imagine the noise! (*D. Loveday*)

An immaculate Midland Compound 4–4–0 no. (4)1167 is admired by staff at Camden goods depot as she tops Camden Bank in this undated picture.

'The Lakes Express' in the charge of no. 46167 *The Hertfordshire Regiment*, pictured at the same location in July 1962. The driver cannot resist a glance across the line to 1B. (*D. Loveday*)

Another Camden Bank scene in July 1962 as no. 46238 *City of Carlisle* lifts her express away from the bank on a Down working. Young enthusiasts often become confused by the fact that southwards to the capital is referred to as an Up working, and a train travelling north as a Down train; common sense to a railwayman, but not to young spotters. (*D. Loveday*)

Princess Coronation class no. 46236 *City of Bradford* heads the 'Merseyside Express' to Liverpool Lime Street, July 1962. Originally streamlined, this engine took part in the 1948 locomotive trials. Her appearance at that time displayed the cut-away on the smokebox; to my generation this gave the class the nickname 'Semi'. For some strange reason we assumed the angled look had some bearing on the streamlining! (*D. Loveday*)

Royal Scot no. 46169 *The Boy Scout* on a Down express, July 1962. The first coach is vintage stock, while the second shows a now forbidden delight – an enthusiast hangs out of the window, having watched a Duchess backing off shed to join her train. (*D. Loveday*)

In its original condition, Patriot no. 45547 gets into its stride as it passes Camden goods depot on 28 February 1959. The bridge in the background gives access to 1B without risking injury from Up trains coasting to their journey's end. (*L.G. Marshall/ R.S. Collection*)

Close to Camden shed Stanier 2–6–4T no. 42606 runs light engine, June 1963. (*D. Loveday*)

Opposite, top: One of the powerful Stanier 2–6–4 tank engines, no. 42482, makes good progress on 28 February 1959.

Opposite, bottom: No. 42367, a Fowler 2–6–4T, running light engine, July 1962. The crew of this Willesden-based locomotive take pride in the photographer's interest in their work. (*D. Loveday*)

First Sight of Camden Shed

A typical first glimpse of Camden shed with a variety of locomotives on show: Princess Coronation class no. 46242 *City of Glasgow*, a Britannia (probably a Longsight (9A) engine), a Royal Scot and a Jinty simmer at the front end of the depot.

At the rear of the depot no fewer than four Stanier Pacifics are to be seen in company with a Britannia, May 1963. On the left no. 46246 *City of Manchester* appears to be out of use as her chimney is covered with sacking. The two Pacifics on the right have ex-streamlined tenders. (*D. Loveday*)

Royal Scot no. 46166 *London Rifle Brigade* is fully loaded with 9 tons of coal, ready for duty. In front of the locomotive can be seen mineral wagons under the ash disposal plant situated at the south end of the depot.

The ex-streamlined Princess Coronation class no. 46238 *City of Carlisle* is coaled up ready for her next run. The tender gives a clue as to her origins. Rebuilds had long side-sheets, no steps at the rear and a tender ladder.

Around London Euston

Some enthusiasts like to observe activities from the side of the line, watching locomotives either trundling or flying past and enduring the periods of inactivity in between, while others prefer station activities, admiring the engines at close range. Station activities offer numerous opportunities to witness the hustle and bustle of express departures and to get close to the locomotives as they arrive.

Euston station opened on 20 July 1837. It is best remembered for the Grand Arch Entrance (in reality the exit), the gatehouse and Hardwick's impressive Great Hall. The name Euston derives from the name of the landowners from whom the site was purchased. In common with many stations in the 1950s and 1960s Euston looks in need of a good clean and even renovation in some areas.

There are fifteen platforms and a hidden-away turntable at Euston, but the best places for spotters are platforms one and two on the arrivals side. Here, they watch the majestic Duchesses, Royal Scots, Jubilees and Princess class locomotives drawing up at the buffer stops to complete their journeys. The curvature of the roof and the sweep of the platforms produce ideal photographs, although piles of parcels often clutters up platform one, together with the parcels vehicles of differing vintage. Taxi ranks are situated between platforms two and three, producing a seemingly endless line of black cabs awaiting fares from rail passengers who have just arrived.

Advertisements feature around the buffer barrier enclosures on platforms one and two, and on the Phoenix Assurance Company clock. Enamel signs affixed to the walls advertise the merits of Palethorpes Royal Cambridge Sausages and Stephens' Inks – a favourite with schoolboys for making ink pellets to be launched at victims with a 12-in ruler!

At the country end of platforms one and two photographers capture superb panoramas of arrivals, with the road bridge forming a backdrop. At times a flowerbed also contributes a dash of colour.

The centre of the station houses a mixture of traffic, including suburban Watford electrics and parcels trains. Platform six is used for occasional royal workings. The stationmaster's office is situated here. The far side of the station is devoted to departures. This is not the greatest photographic location, as it does not afford the distance needed to ensure a good picture.

A Typical Mid-1950s Euston Morning of Principal Trains

Departures					Arrivals			
0.02	Crewe	5A	RS					
0.20	Glasgow	1B	D					
0.30	Liverpool	8A	PR					
0.40	Manchester	8A	J					
					1.10	Crewe	5A	RS
1.37	Wolverhampton	9A	J		1.37	Birmingham	1B	J
					2.40	Liverpool	8A	PR
					3.04	Manchester	9A	RS
					3.32	Windermere	1B	RS
					4.00	Glasgow	5A	RS
					4.30	Kendal	5A	RS
					5.05	Glasgow	1B	RS
					5.24	Manchester	9A	RS
					5.57	Liverpool	8A	RS
					6.30	Holyhead	7C	RS
					6.50	Glasgow	12A	D
					7.03	Glasgow	1B	D
					7.13	Perth	1B	RS
					7.20	Glasgow	1B	D
7.55	Liverpool	1B	D					
					8.05	Stranraer	1B	RS
					8.20	Inverness	5A	D
8.30	Manchester	9A	RS					
8.50	Wolverhampton	1B	J					
9.00	Wolverhampton	3A	J					
9.45	Manchester	9A	RS					
					9.56	Wolverhampton	3A	J
10.00	Glasgow	1B	D					
					10.30	Wolverhampton	3A	J
10.40	Carlisle	1B	D					
10.50	Blackpool	1B	RS					
					11.09	Crewe	5A	D
					11.25	Manchester	9A	RS
					11.35	Heysham	1B	RS
11.45	Manchester	9A	RS					

KEY TO SHEDS
1B Camden · 3A Bushbury · 5A Crewe · 7C Holyhead · 8A Edge Hill
9A Longsight · 12A Carlisle Upperby · 24E Blackpool

KEY TO LOCOMOTIVE CLASSES
D: Duchess · PR: Princess Royal · J: Jubilee · RS: Royal Scot

As the BR Standard classes emerged they were introduced on some services.

Afternoon Principal Services

Departures					Arrivals			
					12.00	Liverpool	8A	PR
12.30	Liverpool	8A	PR					
					12.41	Wolverhampton	3A	J
					12.48	Manchester	9A	RS
12.50	Wolverhampton	3A	J					
					12.55	Blackpool	1B	RS
					13.05	Manchester	9A	RS
					13.20	Holyhead	7C	RS
13.30	Glasgow	5A	D		13.30	Wolverhampton	3A	J
13.35	Blackpool	24E	J					
					13.45	Liverpool	8A	PR
					13.55	Manchester	9A	RS
14.20	Wolverhampton	3A	J					
14.30	Liverpool	8A	RS		14.30	Wolverhampton	3A	J
14.45	Manchester	9A	RS		14.45	Liverpool	8A	J
15.00	Birmingham	1B	J					
					15.05	Blackpool	1B	J
					15.37	Llandudno	5A	J
15.45	Manchester	9A	J		15.45	Manchester	9A	J
					16.12	Carlisle	1B	D
16.30	Manchester	1B	RS					
					16.34	Wolverhampton	1B	J
16.37	Wolverhampton	3A	J					
16.55	Liverpool	8A	RS					
17.05	Blackpool	1B	RS					
					17.15	Glasgow	1B	D
17.35	Holyhead	5A	RS					
					17.45	Liverpool	8A	RS
17.50	Wolverhampton	3A	J					
					17.54	Manchester	9A	RS

Evening Principal Services

Departures					Arrivals			
					18.00	Manchester	9A	RS
					18.10	Liverpool	8A	PR
					18.20	Heysham	1B	RS
18.30	Wolverhampton	1B	J		18.30	Preston	5A	D
					18.55	Wolverhampton	3A	J
					19.00	Birmingham	5A	RS
					19.20	Inverness	1B	RS
19.26	Perth	1B	D					
					19.30	Perth	1B	D
19.52	Manchester	9A	RS					
20.20	Liverpool	8A	RS					
					20.30	Glasgow Travelling Post Office	5A	D
20.50	Liverpool	1B	D		20.50	Holyhead	7C	RS
21.00	Glasgow	1B	D					
					21.10	Glasgow	1B	D
21.20	Manchester	9A	RS					
					21.25	Glasgow	12A	D
					21.35	Birmingham	1B	J
					22.00	Manchester	9A	RS
					22.45	Manchester	9A	RS
					22.52	Perth	7C	RS
23.04	Blackpool	24E	J					
					23.05	Windermere	5A	J
					23.50	Glasgow	1B	RS

Titled Trains

London Euston was the principal station on the London Midland Region and it provided sights of numerous named trains on both Up and Down workings. Scottish services included 'The Royal Scot', 'The Mid-Day Scot' and 'The Caledonian' to and from Glasgow Central. 'The Royal Highlander' reached other parts of Scotland on its journey to Inverness. 'The Northern Irishman' was a feeder train to Stranraer harbour for sailings to Larne in Northern Ireland.

Manchester London Road was the destination of 'The Mancunian', 'The Lancastrian' and 'Comet', while the oldest named train of all, 'The Irish Mail', and 'The Emerald Isle Express' favoured the port of Holyhead.

'The Midlander' provided a good two-hour express service to Birmingham New Street and Wolverhampton High Level. 'The Merseyside Express', 'The Red Rose', 'The Shamrock' and 'The Manxman' were all Liverpool Lime Street services. Liverpool's Riverside station also had services named 'The Empress Voyager' and 'The Cunard Express', which ran as required to connect with sailings of transatlantic liners.

Another port, Heysham, was the destination of 'The Ulster Express', while the North Wales towns of Llandudno, Bangor, Pwllheli and Portmadoc were the destinations of 'The Welshman'. The Lake District was served by 'The Lakes Express', portioned to Keswick, Workington and Windermere.

Express Headboards

During early BR years named expresses carried special headboards intended to adorn the locomotive. These boards were fixed above the smokebox numbers. They were made of aluminium and their backgrounds varied in colour. Some were red and some black, while Scottish versions were blue. 'The Royal Scot' used them all, including a tartan-backed rectangular design with a lion rampant. 'The Caledonian' had its own headboard with the shields of St Andrew and St George above. On this headboard the background colour was red.

'The Caledonian' headboard on display at the National Railway Museum. This train was nearly always working for a Duchess locomotive. There were only two exceptions, when 'Princess Royal' no. 46211 *Queen Maud* and rebuilt Jubilee no. 45736 *Phoenix* were late substitutes for the normal motive power.

Nameplates

One of my earliest memories is of gazing in admiration at Royal Scot no. 46127's nameplate, which had crossed swords on a circular background. How many of us knew who The Old Contemptibles were, and the significance of the dates 5 August to 22 November 1914? For those who never found out, 'Old Contemptibles' was the nickname given to the British Expeditionary Force by the German Kaiser, whose own forces were thwarted by British heroics between those dates.

The joy of underlining a 'namer' in your *abc* was what life revolved around. Names of ex-LMS engines were a geography and history lesson in themselves. The Jubilee class celebrated Commonwealth countries, admirals and famous old warships. The Royal Scots were named in honour of regiments that fought in the First World War, with four exceptions: *The Royal Air Force, The Girl Guide, The Boy Scout* and *British Legion*, with its extremely ornate badge.

The unique nameplate removed from Royal Scot no. 46170 *British Legion* is now on display at the National Railway Museum at York.

A fine display of nameplates was organised by Sheffield Railwayana Auctions for a Crewe Works open day. Both Jubilee and Patriot classes were well represented.

Patriots were predominantly named after regiments, railway company directors and seaside towns on the LMS system. Also honoured were some railway employees who had been awarded the VC in the First World War. Indeed, the very first example, no. 45500 *Patriot*, was named in honour of the dead of that war.

The nameplates used on LMS engines were made of brass. Most, with the exception of the Duchesses, were curved to suit the profile of the wheelsplashers on which they were mounted. Sizes varied. Short names such as *Phoenix* were 29in long, while increasing sizes of 35, 42, 48, 52 and 56in were required to accommodate the longer names of the Royal Scots. Some of these even required double lines. Attractive crests or badges were sometimes built into the backing plates of some nameplates, usually above the name, while several nameplates had these extras displayed on the wheelsplasher itself.

All thirteen members of the Princess Royal class carried names, mainly of Queen Victoria's children, and the present queen and her sister in the shape of no. 46201 *Princess Elizabeth* and no. 46203 *Princess Margaret Rose*. These two were the only examples of the class to escape the scrapyard, to the delight of many enthusiasts. No. 46202 was built with a turbine drive and was nicknamed the Turbomotive. Rebuilt as a conventional engine in 1952, it was then renamed *Princess Anne*. The names *Princess Arthur of Connaught* and *Queen Maud* were confusing for young minds, and I often wondered why the name *Duchess of Kent* had not been bestowed on a Duchess locomotive.

An impressive selection of Princess Royal and Princess Coronation locomotive nameplates displayed at the Crewe works open day.

All the Duchess engines bore long straight nameplates in the same style. During their early service some of these engines had chrome-plated examples, but this did not last and the chrome was removed before BR days. The smallest LMS nameplate, really a badge about 18in long, was that fitted to Patriot no. 45501 *St. Dunstan's*, while one of the largest was that of no. 46254 *City of Stoke-on-Trent* at about 7ft 6in long – quite a contrast.

On an engine's withdrawal from service the nameplates would be removed. In most instances one plate would be donated to the city, regiment or town commemorated by the name while the other was offered for sale to the public at scrap value. Enthusiasts unofficially removed some plates for souvenirs. I hope none went into the melting pot. Auction prices today for such souvenirs attract very high bidding; for example, upwards of £30,000 was paid for a nameplate from no. 46243 *City of Lancaster*.

A sample of the Duchess nameplates on show at Crewe. *Coronation, King George VI* and *Queen Mary* appear to have been rechromed in preservation.

'The Ulster Express', powered by Royal Scot no. 46154 *The Hussar*, approaches Euston's platform one with a train from Heysham in 1954.

4. Arrivals at London Euston

With just 300yd to go to complete the 401-mile journey from Glasgow, no. 46239 *City of Chester* heads 'The Caledonian' into the Euston complex in about 1957. (*P.H. Groom*)

'The Midlander' train operates between Wolverhampton/Birmingham New Street and Euston, hauled mostly by Bushbury Jubilee class engines. The train's two-hour timings require hard work and quick turn-arounds. The normal well-turned-out appearance of a Bushbury Jubilee is illustrated by no. 45741 *Leinster* as it draws the train to the end of its journey. This engine later moved to Carlisle. Withdrawn from service in early 1964, it was scrapped a few months later.

Opposite, top: No. 45736 *Phoenix*, one of the two rebuilt Jubilee 4–6–0s, approaches Euston's platform two with an Up express. Allocated to Camden, *Phoenix* looks very similar to a rebuilt Royal Scot but closer examination reveals a Stanier-type cab and no steps on the front end.

Opposite, bottom: Original Patriot 4–6–0 no. 45538 *Giggleswick* nicely framed by the road bridge on 1 August 1959.

'The Shamrock' arrives from
Liverpool headed by no. 46208
Princess Helena Victoria of Edge
Hill shed, 11 October 1956.
(R.F. Apwood[?]/R.S. Collection)

Royal Scot no. 46161 *Kings Own* of Manchester Longsight (9A) arrives with 'The Mancunian'. The Euston sign is a welcoming cherry red. *(R.K. Blencowe)*

Another 'Mancunian' arrival, this time headed by no. 46160 *Queen Victoria's Rifleman*. Pencil in hand, the spotter is poised to record the sighting.

Royal Scot no. 46151 *The Royal Horse Guardsman* arrives at platform two with yet another train from Manchester London Road (later known as Piccadilly). Note the sign prohibiting spotters from going beyond the end of the platform.

Royal Scot no. 46131 *Royal Warwickshire Regiment* is based at Longsight. Here it is within sight of journey's end with the Up 'Mancunian'. Locomotive crews regard several of the Royal Scots, including this one, as 'rough riders'.

Headed by Jubilee no. 45734 *Meteor* (with steam shut off), another 'Midlander' arrives on time. Not all the locomotives for this train were based at Bushbury, as Camden depot provided engines for some workings.

This is one of my favourite photographs, with Black Five no. 45395 displaying the first British Railways coat of arms, nicknamed the 'wheel and ferret'.

A favourite engine for many scouts, this is Royal Scot no. 46169 *The Boy Scout*. In keeping with its name, the locomotive is quite smartly turned out. The same cannot be said of the station's canopy paintwork.

The only unnamed Britannia, no. 70047, arrives alongside platform three, observed by an enthusiast. The Britannias were the first Standard class to appear, with the first example, no. 70000 *Britannia,* being completed at Crewe works in early 1951. In all, fifty-five were built, and all carried names except for no. 70047.

Another Royal Scot with a reputation for rough riding is no. 46122 *The Royal Ulster Rifleman*, seen here passing spotters relaxing against the canopy column. The Royal Scots based at Longsight are usually to be seen heading most of the London–Manchester services in the 1950s.

Rebuilt Patriot no. 45530 *Sir Frank Ree* enters Euston under the watchful gaze of boys at the platform ends. Their style of dress – school cap, raincoat and satchel is now a thing of the past. This engine was built in 1933 and rebuilt with a taper boiler in 1947.

Camden-based Jubilee no. 45606 *Falkland Islands* rounds the curve into the station. In those days few of us had heard of the Falklands. Sadly this was to change in the 1980s.

A Vulcan Foundry Black Five, no. 45091, built in 1935 with combined top-feed and dome, steams in with a parcels train for Euston. The working is probably from Northampton, judging by the 2E shed code.

Jubilee no. 45647 *Sturdee* eases into Euston with what looks like 'The Midlander'.

Jubilee no. 45592 *Indore* heads inwards with a rake of ex-LMS Stanier coaches in May 1960. Spotters cluster by the notice warning them not to venture past the board.

Royal Scot no. 46155 *The Lancer*. By 1963 this engine was one of several Royal Scots allocated to Llandudno Junction depot. A Derby-built engine, it was completed in 1930 and withdrawn in late 1964 for scrapping.

One of the new generation of Pacifics, Britannia no. 70044 *Earl Haig* is admired by the young spotters on the platform. This was one of two Britannias to be fitted with Westinghouse pumps for trials with fast air-braked freight trains. The other was no. 70043 *Lord Kitchener*.

Euston Station Activities

Once a train had arrived young spotters would gaze at its locomotive admiringly, all hoping to be allowed up on the footplate. This never seemed to be allowed at the bigger stations. Some of the arriving passengers headed for the taxi rank and others for the nearest exit, while staff would set to work unloading some of the huge amounts of parcels that entered Euston each day. Porters suddenly appeared for the arrival of an express, hoping to earn tips for their efficient service with the passengers' luggage. They would disappear just as quickly once the passengers had dispersed.

If the incoming locomotive had been stationary for a time, an event would occur that terrified most young spotters (and passengers). The driver would open the drain cocks on the cylinders, resulting in a loud roar and clouds of steam escaping from the front of the loco. It was only in science lessons later that we learned how steam turns to water, and that water does not compress. The driver was not intent on frightening us to death. He was simply preventing damage to the pistons in the cylinders. The driver and those who knew what to expect always enjoyed a good laugh at the expense of those who did not!

When no departures or arrivals were imminent, spotters took the opportunity to look round the station, perhaps paying a visit to the bookstall or the Great Hall or touring the lesser platforms to observe pilot engines slumbering between duties. So numerous were such locomotives in those days that few spotters bothered to observe and record them.

The fireman has time for a cheery word to the spotter as no. 46203 *Princess Margaret Rose* draws gently into Euston.

Here 4–6–0 Patriot no. 45511 *Isle of Man* is taking empty stock from the station to the carriage sidings. During her long career this engine changed shed allocation no fewer than twenty-four times.

The crew of Black Five no. 44909 are happy to be recorded by the photographer.

Stanier 8F no. 48514 moves empty stock past loaded trolleys, 19 September 1959. The inwards parcels office can be seen behind the lorry. The 8F is one of Stanier's best-known and most successful designs. In all, 852 were built, although only 624 were for the LMS. The others went to the War Department during the Second World War, and were to be found as far afield as Iraq and Turkey.

Opposite, top: Black Five no. 45191 passes two of the numerous platform trolleys that are always so much in evidence at Euston. A Standard tank 2–6–4 no. 80065 is also partly visible. (*G.W. Sharpe/R.S. Collection*)

Opposite, bottom: No. 46203 *Princess Margaret Rose* backs out to gain the road back to Camden for servicing.

Stanier 8F no. 48624 of Willesden seen here on empty stock duty on 30 May 1952. The buffer-beam notice 'NEW E' is a mystery.

Spotters are often treated to a little variety at Euston. Here a Fowler-Hughes 'Crab' 2–6–0 moves coaches out, while the driver of Jubilee no. 45666 *Cornwallis* backs on to coaching stock ready for departure. In all 245 'Crabs' were built for the LMS. Powerful and versatile, they prove equally at home on passenger and freight trains. They are easily identifiable by their inclined cylinders.

Shunting is in progress with Jubilee no. 45721 *Impregnable* on very light duties, April 1963. (*D. Loveday*)

A group of elder statesmen from the spotters' fraternity compare notes, seemingly uninterested in the presence of Jinty 0–6–0T no. 47302.

Standard 2–6–0 no. 78039 of Willesden looks very smart as it waits to depart with its coaches from platform two in June 1963. No doubt the fireman thinks he does too, in his highly fashionable tight trousers! The 78000 class engines were derived from the Ivatt 2MT 2–6–0 design first introduced in 1946. Few changes were made, except for the incorporation of BR standard fittings. (*D. Loveday*)

Black Five no. 45389 is one of 327 members of the class constructed by Armstrong-Whitworth.

The arrival of 'The Irish Mail' from Holyhead with no. 46200 *The Princess Royal* in charge. Early diesels can be seen at platforms one and three, and note the ubiquitous black cabs for arriving passengers. 'The Irish Mail' is the oldest named train on British Railways.

The bustle caused by the arrival of parcels is about to commence as the driver of no. 46220 *Coronation* enjoys a brief chat before taking the locomotive on shed, April 1962. (*D. Loveday*)

Rebuilt Patriot no. 45529 *Stephenson* of Crewe North shed (5A) in immaculate external condition arrives at platform two. Built by the LMS in 1933, this engine was originally named *Sir Herbert Walker K.C.B.* It was rebuilt with a taper boiler in July 1947, and renamed *Stephenson* a year later.

Royal Scot no. 46150 *The Life Guardsman* brings 'The Irish Mail' from Holyhead in North Wales safely to its destination.

Opposite, top: Carlisle Upperby-based no. 46244 *King George VI* has her draincocks opened before assisting the pilot engine in pushing the empty stock up Camden Bank.

Opposite, bottom: The bustling of Euston is brilliantly captured in this scene, evoking all the excitement of an express train. 'The Mancunian', headed by Royal Scot no. 46111 *Royal Fusilier*, nears the end of its journey, watched by the crowd of onlookers.

The 8A shedplate identifies no. 46208 *Princess Helena Victoria* as an arrival from Liverpool. On the platform is a Scammell parcels wagon.

Activity on platform two as parcels trolleys are towed into place to unload the newly arrived train headed by Royal Scot no. 46122 *Royal Ulster Rifleman*. An early diesel design, a Deltic-bodied DP2, stands alongside.

Opposite, top: In 1937 the LMS gained the World Steam Speed Record with the streamlined no. 46220 *Coronation* achieving 114mph. This was eclipsed soon afterwards by the LNER with *Mallard*'s record which will probably stand for all time. Now shorn of its 3 tons of streamlined casing, *Coronation* stands at platform one with a sleeper train arrival.

Opposite, bottom: A long sweeping view of Royal Scot no. 46136 *The Border Regiment* and its train. The release points for locomotives using platform one can be clearly seen. This engine is based at Crewe North shed (5A).

Just after lunchtime no. 46248 *City of Leeds* arrives. The volume of parcels that pass through Euston can be judged by the overburdened parcels trolley. This engine was completed in October 1943 and withdrawn from service in 1964 for scrapping.

No. 46235 *City of Birmingham* arrives with an early morning sleeper train at platform one. This engine escaped the scrapman's torch and found a new home at the Birmingham Museum of Science and Industry. It was originally built with streamlining in 1939.

It is now early evening and Royal Scot no. 46168 *The Girl Guide* completes the sequence. Note the ancient parcels lorry just visible on the right. The chequers on the trailer on the far right denote inter-station traffic.

There's a problem. Spotters, a passenger and a locomotive fitter inspect the buffer beam of Royal Scot no. 46143 *The South Staffordshire Regiment*. (*S.V. Blencowe Collection*)

This is an unusual pairing: a Crewe-based 2P 4–4–0 and a Duchess wait at platform two. (*R.K. Blencowe*)

No. 46253 *City of St. Albans* stands alongside a seemingly deserted platform one.

No. 46209 *Princess Beatrice* in close up. An example of the new Watford Electric units waits at the next platform.

Passengers from the newly arrived no. 46234 *Duchess of Abercorn* struggle to manage their luggage during this late afternoon scene.

Another day, another arrival with a sleeper train for no. 46235 *City of Birmingham*. Passengers have alighted leaving the carriage doors open; they will need to be closed before the stock is taken away for cleaning.

In somewhat grimy condition, no. 46206 *Princess Marie Louise* waits to back down to Camden shed, 28 February 1959. The left-side headlamp appears to have nearly fallen off during the journey.

Passengers on their way to work pass no. 46250 *City of Lichfield* arriving with a sleeper service.

This is a sight to thrill young spotters: a pair of Royal Scots double-heading. The driver of the second engine is in conversation with the crew of no. 46131 *The Royal Warwickshire Regiment*, which is based at 6G.

A favourite engine at Crewe North shed is no. 46248 *City of Leeds*, seen here minutes away from backing out of Euston for servicing.

City gents cannot resist glancing at no. 46228 *Duchess of Rutland* with a lunchtime arrival.

Royal Scot no. 46148 *The Manchester Regiment* stops short of the buffers. Now it is the turn of a schoolboy, who cannot resist a second look at the engine. Interest in locomotives bridges all generations.

No. 46246 *City of Manchester* waits to clear the road and back down to Camden. How many people can remember the Pepsodent advertisement slogan that the young lady is smiling about?

Jubilee no. 45681 *Aboukir* at rest platform two. Signs of a spillage are evident on the other platform. The public information sign for refreshments must be one of the most photographed of all as few photographers can resist this ideal location.

No. 46225 *Duchess of Gloucester* alongside platform one, 1962. Built in 1936 with streamlining, this engine was withdrawn from service in 1964, despite still being in fine condition, and taken to Carlisle Upperby for storing. It was subsquently towed to Troon and scrapped. (*D. Loveday*)

A 'classic shot' spoiled! The driver of the unidentified rebuild on the left has opened the cylinder draincocks enveloping the front end of the locomotive in steam. No. 46254 *City of Stoke-on-Trent* has just arrived with 'The Ulster Express'.

Mid-day activity. Arriving passengers stream away from platform two passing no. 46229 *Duchess of Hamilton* heading 'The Ulster Express'. A young boy admires the engine and a crewman explains the valve arrangement to him. On the right is no. 46131 *The Royal Warwickshire Regiment*. (*G. Coltas*)

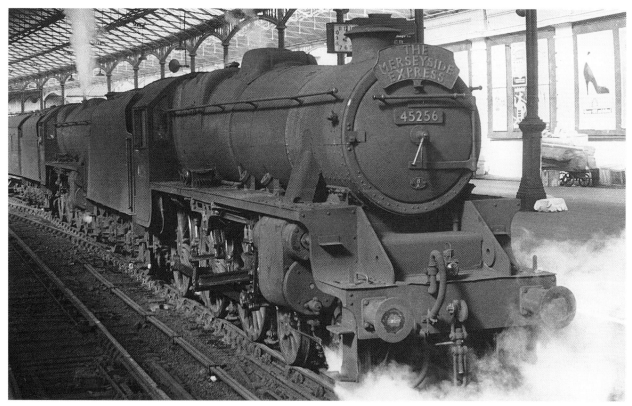

'The Merseyside Express' headed by two Black Fives as no. 45256 pilots a sister locomotive. Normal motive power for the train is a Pacific from Edge Hill (8A).

Stanier Pacific no. 46233 *Duchess of Sutherland*. The fireman can be seen on top of the coal in the tender. This is unusual as the engine is at the end of its journey. In common with all other members of the Princess Coronation class it had a steam-operated coal pusher. This engine has survived into preservation, one of three members of the class to do so.

5. Camden Shed (1B)

Camden has always been a busy shed, with locomotives reversing back from Euston for servicing. In some cases they would assist empty stock up the bank, then drop off and enter the shed at its north end. The locomotives are then turned on the Cowan's Sheldon 70ft turntable to face north before progressing through to the coaling plant to top up their tenders. The coaling plant consists of two 150-ton bunkers, which are replenished at night with good-quality coal. As you might imagine, the noise from this operation is not appreciated by local householders.

After coaling, the tenders are filled with water under one of the numerous water columns on site. Finally, fire-cleaning or disposal takes place using the 25-ton ash plant. The Henry Lees Company constructed both the coaling and ash plants in about 1937.

A real collector's item. Sadly this shedplate is not mine.

Locomotive crews on double home turns make their way to the nearby ninety-bed lodging quarters known as the 'Barracks' to try to get some sleep, although this place has a reputation as the noisiest on the system. After servicing, and possibly cleaning, the locomotives are stabled ready for their next duties. Details of line location and destinations, together with times, are displayed on the large daily arrangements board situated inside the shed.

For some workings a trip has to be made to the stores to collect the appropriate headboard, which then has to be fixed above the smokebox door. Headboards such as 'The Royal Scot' or 'The Mancunian' give a dignified importance to the engine.

Departure off shed is in reverse gear to Euston, with several engines backing down together on occasions to save line occupation. On reaching Euston they are signalled into their allocated platforms to couple ahead of their respective stock, ready for departure.

Special royal workings originating from Euston are code-named 'The Grove'. When such a working is planned, two Pacific locomotives are cleaned to perfection. The allocated locomotive has its buffers and drawbar hook removed and replaced with a special burnished set provided by Crewe Works. The other cleaned Pacific is kept on stand-by in case of problems. A new set of overalls is issued to the crew for the occasion and a locomotive will have gone to Wolverton to pick up the royal train stock in readiness. To drive a royal train with a four-headlamp code is a great honour for the crew. After the event, a 'Thank You' letter from the management becomes a treasured item for all those involved.

On Remembrance Day, in keeping with several other depots, Camden staff display poppies on some departing train locomotives in honour of the war dead.

No. 46200 *The Princess Royal* at Camden shed, turning to back through the shed yard for servicing. The engine is one of the few in the class to receive the red livery intended for daytime use; because of expense the night workers retain their Brunswick green livery.

The driver of no. 46246 *City of Manchester* turns his locomotive using its vacuum system connected to the turntable, July 1962. (*D. Loveday*)

No. 46131 *The Royal Warwickshire Regiment* is turned after arrival with 'The Mancunian'.

No. 46240 *City of Coventry* appears to be receiving a good clean for royal duties, July 1962. The special set of burnished buffers is in evidence, together with another Pacific about to be cleaned. This engine was allocated to Camden. It entered service in 1940 and was withdrawn in 1964 for scrapping. (*D. Loveday*)

Record-breaker no. 46220 *Coronation* makes its way through the shed servicing facilities, April 1962. It has just passed under the footbridge leading from the entrance to the depot. (*D. Loveday*)

Still displaying its express headlamp coding, *Coronation* progresses through the depot, drawing back to the ash plant in the background . . . (*D. Loveday*)

. . . and passes under the coaling plant. Around 10 tons of coal will be dropped into her tender ready for her next working. For an engine that will be on shed for several hours yet, a little too much steam pressure is evident. (*D. Loveday*)

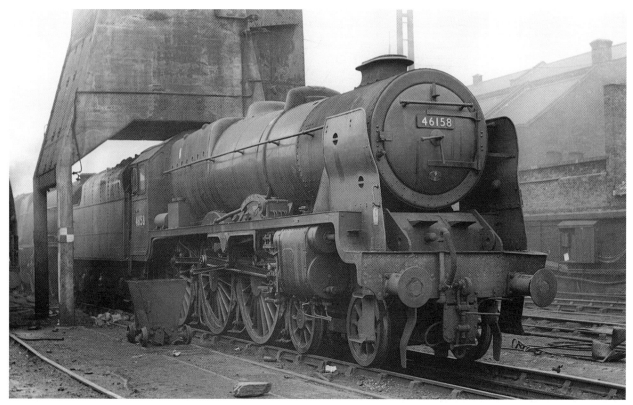

Royal Scot no. 46158 *The Loyal Regiment* of Longsight shed (9A) shows signs of heavy damage to her buffer beam, July 1962. *(D. Loveday)*

A sight to thrill all spotters, this is no. 46256 *Sir William A. Stanier F.R.S.*, pictured at Camden in June 1963. Built during the Ivatt period, it was named in 1947 after the man responsible for the production of so many fine LMS designs. *(D. Loveday)*

Jubilee no. 45705 *Seahorse*, disfigured by a scruffy chalked identity, is in the company of a Duchess and several diesels in July 1962. My first sighting of no. 45705 was at Bloomfield Road, Blackpool, where I had to choose between watching Sir Stanley Matthews playing football or *Seahorse* on shed at 24E. *(D. Loveday)*

Royal Scot no. 46162 *Queen's Westminster Rifleman* has only a Duchess for company as the diesels start to take over the steam workings.

It's July 1962 and no. 46238 *City of Carlisle*, of Carlisle Upperby shed (12A), displays the headboard for 'The Caledonian', an eight-coach limited load express introduced in 1957. This headboard deserves a second look, as it is a much smaller version of the better known one. *(D. Loveday)*

The pride of Camden, Princess Coronation class no. 46245 *City of London* was named at Euston on 20 July 1943. Coincidentally Euston station itself opened on the same date in 1837. *City of London* was the first locomotive to receive the smart red livery applied to some Duchesses and Princesses in January 1958. It is seen here in June 1963 in very smart condition. *(D. Loveday)*

The presence in Camden in April 1962 of Jubilee no. 45660 *Rooke* from 89A Oswestry shed is a mystery. Britannia no. 70033 *Charles Dickens* is easier to explain as it worked in from Manchester on a regular basis. It was an appropriate choice of name as Dickens himself resided in the Camden area for some years. *(D. Loveday)* NO is Shrewsbury loco!

The enormity of no. 46244 *King George VI* is seen in this incomplete view of the locomotive on Camden's turntable. Its driving wheels are 6ft 9in in diameter, so the nameplate must be about 7ft long.

No. 46239 *City of Chester* alongside the ash plant, April 1962. Note the small wagon on the narrow gauge rails alongside; this is used for fire disposal. (*D. Loveday*)

Jubilee no. 45669 *Fisher* prepares to take 'The Royal Highlander' onwards to Inverness, July 1962. The train should undergo several engine changes on route, the first probably at Crewe where *Fisher* could be replaced with a fresh locomotive. (*D. Loveday*)

Jubilee no. 45721 *Impregnable* at the rear of Camden shed in April 1962. This engine is allocated to Crewe North shed (5A). To the right are 16-ton mineral wagons under the ash plant, for filling and disposal. The lower view shows the close proximity of homes. *(D. Loveday)*

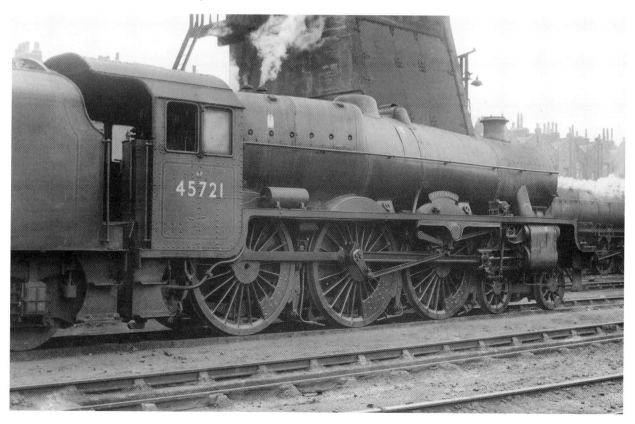

No. 46209 *Princess Beatrice* under the coaling stage in April 1962, about to receive a 10-ton top-up. Once again there seems to be a little too much steam pressure for an engine on shed. *(D. Loveday)*

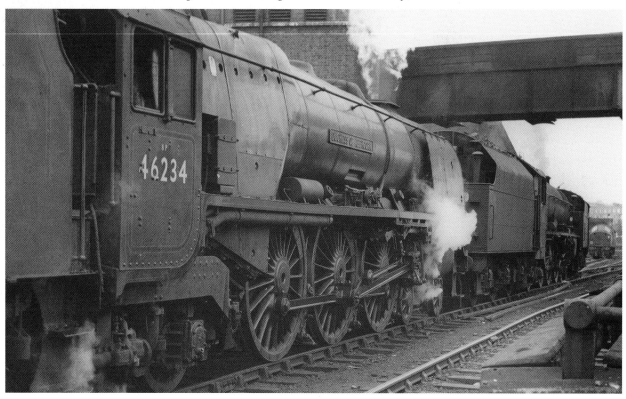

Three Stanier engines coupled together for the short trip to Euston, in July 1962. The two nearest the camera are no. 46234 *Duchess of Abercorn* (in green livery) and no. 46206 *Princess Marie Louise* (identified as the only member of her class fitted with a tender coal pusher). The third engine is a Stanier design but could be any of the 4–6–0 classes. *(D. Loveday)*

6. Departures from London Euston

The driver of no. 46206 *Princess Marie Louise* oils the lubricators in readiness for departure with 'The Mid-Day Scot'. (*Travel Lens Photographic*)

Jubilee no. 45721 *Impregnable* makes a positive start with 'The Midlander' and overtakes a Fowler 2–6–2 tank engine which is removing empty stock.

Royal Scot no. 46126 *Royal Army Service Corps* attracts only a passing glance. On the right of the picture two early design diesels are on duty.

Double-heading, with Black Five no. 44831 leading an unidentified Stanier design, April 1962. (*D. Loveday*)

An admirer enjoys a close-up inspection of no. 46204 *Princess Louise*. The well-kept flowerbed provides a dash of colour. This engine was one of six Princess Royals to be withdrawn from service in 1961. (*G. Coltas*)

Duchess no. 46239 *City of Chester* prepares to leave Euston in June 1963. Could the canopy be a prototype of some modern station designs? (*D. Loveday*)

A nicely turned out Black Five, no. 45393, takes the strain as it eases its train out of Euston. (*G.W. Sharpe/R.S. Collection*)

Although the smokebox number is hidden, this Royal Scot is no. 46110 *Grenadier Guardsman*, pictured in April 1963. (*D. Loveday*)

No. 46203 *Princess Margaret Rose* simmering from its safety valves as the driver waits for the guard's signal. Young spotters admire the locomotive from close range; note the shorts and school cap.

Although no. 46170 *British Legion* looks like every other Royal Scot, it differs in several ways, notably having a longer boiler and Stanier-type cab. Here the locomotive is admired by a group of spotters, one of whom is obscuring the ornate lion's head nameplate. The flowerbed is planted with geraniums.

The crew of a very dirty Black Five, no. 45387, enjoy a few minutes' rest before departure piloting one of the early diesels, 1960.

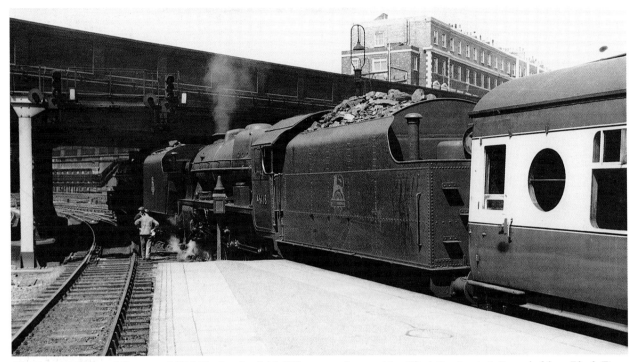

The drivers of Royal Scot no. 46138 *The London Irish Rifleman* and an unidentified Stanier 4–6–0, probably a Black Five, discuss the details of the forthcoming trip. No. 46138 was built in 1927 as *Fury*; it was renamed in 1929.

Judging by the lamp positioned by the tender, it appears that no. 46155 *The Lancer* is backing on to her train and coupling up ready for departure. A Derby-built engine, *The Lancer* entered service in 1930 and was withdrawn in December 1964.

Flashback to the 1930s and an immaculate no. 6221 *Queen Elizabeth* in streamlined form is on a Down train. The engine's livery stripes continued along the articulated coaches for the full length of the train. (*L.J. Burley*)

Thirty years later and the road overbridge has been demolished to prepare for the rebuilding of Euston. Willesden-based Jubilee no. 45704 *Leviathan* is on empty carriage stock removal duties on 29 July 1964.

Rebuilt Patriot no. 45530 *Sir Frank Ree* awaits the guard's flag for departure to Liverpool with 'The Shamrock'. In all, eighteen 7P rebuilds were constructed, including *Sir Frank Ree*. This was the last of the class in service, and was withdrawn in December 1965. (*R.S. Carpenter/R.S. Collection*)

Edge Hill-based Royal Scot no. 46153 *The Royal Dragoon* is ten minutes away from its 4.55 departure time with 'The Shamrock' on its inaugural train to Liverpool.

A stirring Euston departure with no. 46256 *Sir William A. Stanier, F.R.S.* in charge of a Birmingham express, 10 March 1963. (*P.H. Groom*)

The Missing 'Princess'

One number that was not in our *abc* spotter's book was that of 'Princess Royal' no. (4)6202. This was a unique engine that proved to be very successful, but it was doomed by the events of war and a horrific rail crash. Known as the Turbomotive, it entered LMS service in 1935. Its 6ft 6in wheels, boiler and cab were the same as on the other Princess engines but here the similarities ended, as no. 6202 was fitted with two turbines developed by the Metropolitan Vickers Company.

The larger turbine was for forward movement, the smaller for reverse. With normal 3- or 4-cylinder locomotives, hammer blows are transmitted to the track at a rate of 3 or 4 times per wheel revolution, i.e. every 120 degrees or 90 degrees. In contrast, the Turbomotive had power input throughout 360 degrees of wheel revolution, hence delivering no hammer blows whatever. Control was a simple matter of opening the regulator as an on/off switch and progressive opening of six valves to achieve full power. As express engines do not normally travel in service in reverse, the small turbine did not produce large power outputs.

A double chimney was fitted from new to the loco, which resulted in a very soft blast, necessitating the fitting of smoke deflectors to give clearer forward vision to the engine crew. In this form no. 6202 performed very satisfactorily on mainly Liverpool–Euston expresses, but because of its uniqueness a fitter always travelled on board as part of the crew to oversee mechanical maintenance. Unfortunately, lubrication problems plagued the Turbomotive, which resulted in a series of lengthy works visits while spares were manufactured.

During the Second World War spares became a major concern. Metropolitan Vickers was committed to the war effort, so one-off replacements for complex components proved nearly impossible to obtain. By the late 1940s a new main turbine was required. This was deemed too expensive so the engine was rebuilt as a conventional reciprocating engine. What emerged from the works in August 1952 was a hybrid of both Princess and Duchess designs, and as no. 46202 it received the name *Princess Anne*. Subsequently it returned to her once-regular workings between Liverpool and Euston. Sadly its career was cut short in October 1952 when it was involved in the horrific Harrow and Wealdstone disaster. Deemed too badly damaged to repair, it never returned to service. Its boiler was salvaged and taken into stock, and later saw service on other members of the class. Its tender (unique in having straight steps) was attached to an 8F and would have been scrapped along with the 8F in the late 1960s. The engine's nameplates are still displayed on occasions.

TURBINE-DRIVEN LOCOMOTIVE, L.M.S.R.

7. Reflections

After a trip like this, the prospect of recording our sightings neatly in our *abc* books would keep us entertained on the return trip. A lot of observations would be new, but some would not. Strangely the Standard BR designs do not seem to have really made their mark on services and ex-LMS engines are still the main motive power on view.

Of the trains spotted on this journey only nos 45231, 46203, 46229, 46233 and 46235 are still in existence. All the others were reduced to scrap. Luckily for enthusiasts, Birmingham Corporation took the opportunity to purchase no. 46235 *City of Birmingham* to become a museum exhibit in the city. The other Pacifics survived because Sir Billy Butlin had the foresight to purchase them as attractions for his holiday camps. Many items such as nameplates, smokebox numbers and shedplates found their way into the hands of collectors if they were not required for official presentation to cities, regiments or other institutions.

Euston station has been reconstructed but it retains none of its old structure or its character. The locomotive shed of Camden closed down and is no more, like numerous other depots. It is fortunate that many of the scenes of yesteryear have been captured on film for us to enjoy. In contrast, Crewe is still recognisable, although changed in layout. The locomotive works there is now in private ownership.

Fortunately open days often feature good selections of preserved engines and the thousands who attend such events can savour once again the sights and smells of steam and hot oil.

No. 46249 *City of Sheffield* departs with 'The Mid-Day Scot'. Farewell to steam.